This Journal Belongs To:

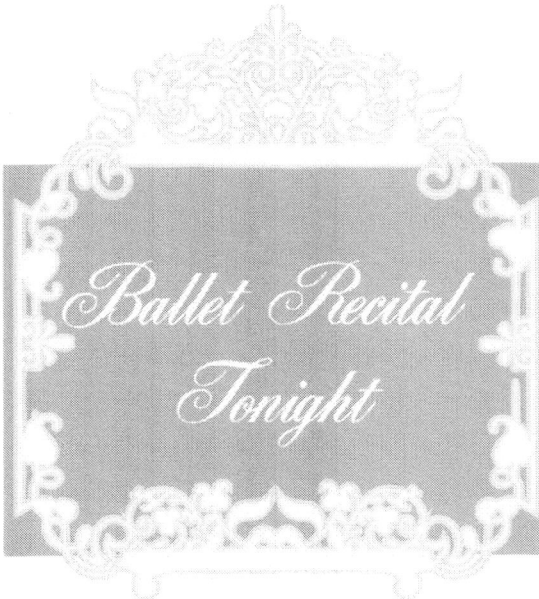

....

Ballet Recital
Tonight

When I Dance – I Feel....

My Dancing Goals

GOAL:	What Do I Need To Do:	✓

GOAL:	What Do I Need To Do:	✓

GOAL:	What Do I Need To Do:	✓

Weekly Dance Plan

MON:

TUE:

WED:

THUR:

FRI:

SAT:

SUN:

PREPARATION

NOTES

THOUGHTS

My Lesson

LESSON DATE:

TEACHER:

ROUTINE:

LESSON FOCUS:

RESULTS: ✓

WHAT WENT WELL:

THINGS I NEED TO WORK ON:

My Practice Plan

MON	
TUE	
WED	
THUR	
FRI	
SAT	
SUN	

My Dance Practice

DATE

ROUTINE:

WHAT TO FOCUS ON:

WHAT WAS GOING WELL:

FEELINGS ABOUT ROUTINE:

WHERE DO I NEED TO IMPROVE:

NOTES:

THOUGHTS AND REFELECTIONS:

My Dance Practice

DATE

WHAT TO FOCUS ON:

FEELINGS ABOUT ROUTINE:

THOUGHTS AND REFELECTIONS:

ROUTINE:

WHAT WAS GOING WELL:

WHERE DO I NEED TO IMPROVE:

NOTES:

My Dance Practice

DATE

ROUTINE:

WHAT TO FOCUS ON:

WHAT WAS GOING WELL:

WHERE DO I NEED TO IMPROVE:

FEELINGS ABOUT ROUTINE:

NOTES:

THOUGHTS AND REFELECTIONS:

My Dance Practice

DATE

WHAT TO FOCUS ON:

FEELINGS ABOUT ROUTINE:

THOUGHTS AND REFELECTIONS:

ROUTINE:

WHAT WAS GOING WELL:

WHERE DO I NEED TO IMPROVE:

NOTES:

Self-Care Planner

TASKS & ERRANDS
MON:
TUES:
WED:
THUR:
FRI:
SAT:
SUN:

TO DO LIST:

NOTES & REMINDERS

THOUGHTS

Future Goals

WHEN	MY GOALS	STEPS
6 MONTHS		
1 YEAR		
2 YEARS		
5 YEARS		

WHERE I CAN DRAW INSPIRATION FROM:

Checklist

FOR: DATE: ✓

NOTES:

I love Dance Because..

My Dancing Goals

GOAL:	What Do I Need To Do:	✔

GOAL:	What Do I Need To Do:	✔

GOAL:	What Do I Need To Do:	✔

Weekly Dance Plan

MON:

TUE:

WED:

THUR:

FRI:

SAT:

SUN:

PREPARATION

NOTES

THOUGHTS

My Lesson

LESSON DATE:

TEACHER:

ROUTINE:

LESSON FOCUS:

RESULTS: ✓

WHAT WENT WELL:

THINGS I NEED TO WORK ON:

My Practice Plan

MON	
TUE	
WED	
THUR	
FRI	
SAT	
SUN	

My Dance Practice

DATE

ROUTINE:

WHAT TO FOCUS ON:

WHAT WAS GOING WELL:

FEELINGS ABOUT ROUTINE:

WHERE DO I NEED TO IMPROVE:

NOTES:

THOUGHTS AND REFELECTIONS:

My Dance Practice

DATE

ROUTINE:

WHAT TO FOCUS ON:

WHAT WAS GOING WELL:

FEELINGS ABOUT ROUTINE:

WHERE DO I NEED TO IMPROVE:

NOTES:

THOUGHTS AND REFELECTIONS:

My Dance Practice

DATE

WHAT TO FOCUS ON:

FEELINGS ABOUT ROUTINE:

THOUGHTS AND REFELECTIONS:

ROUTINE:

WHAT WAS GOING WELL:

WHERE DO I NEED TO IMPROVE:

NOTES:

My Dance Practice

DATE

ROUTINE:

WHAT TO FOCUS ON:

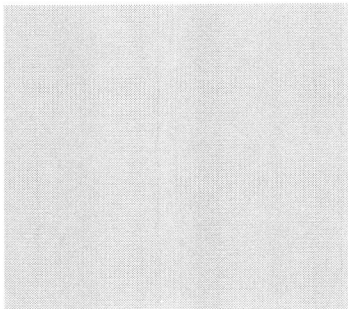

WHAT WAS GOING WELL:

FEELINGS ABOUT ROUTINE:

WHERE DO I NEED TO IMPROVE:

NOTES:

THOUGHTS AND REFELECTIONS:

Self-Care Planner

TASKS & ERRANDS
MON:
TUES:
WED:
THUR:
FRI:
SAT:
SUN:

TO DO LIST:

☐
☐
☐
☐
☐
☐
☐
☐
☐
☐

NOTES & REMINDERS

THOUGHTS

Future Goals

WHEN	MY GOALS	STEPS
6 MONTHS		
1 YEAR		
2 YEARS		
5 YEARS		

WHERE I CAN DRAW INSPIRATION FROM:

Checklist

FOR: _____   DATE: _____   ✓

_____	_____ ▢
_____	_____ ▢
_____	_____ ▢
_____	_____ ▢
_____	_____ ▢
_____	_____ ▢
_____	_____ ▢
_____	_____ ▢
_____	_____ ▢
_____	_____ ▢
_____	_____ ▢
_____	_____ ▢
_____	_____ ▢
_____	_____ ▢

NOTES:

I love Dance Because..

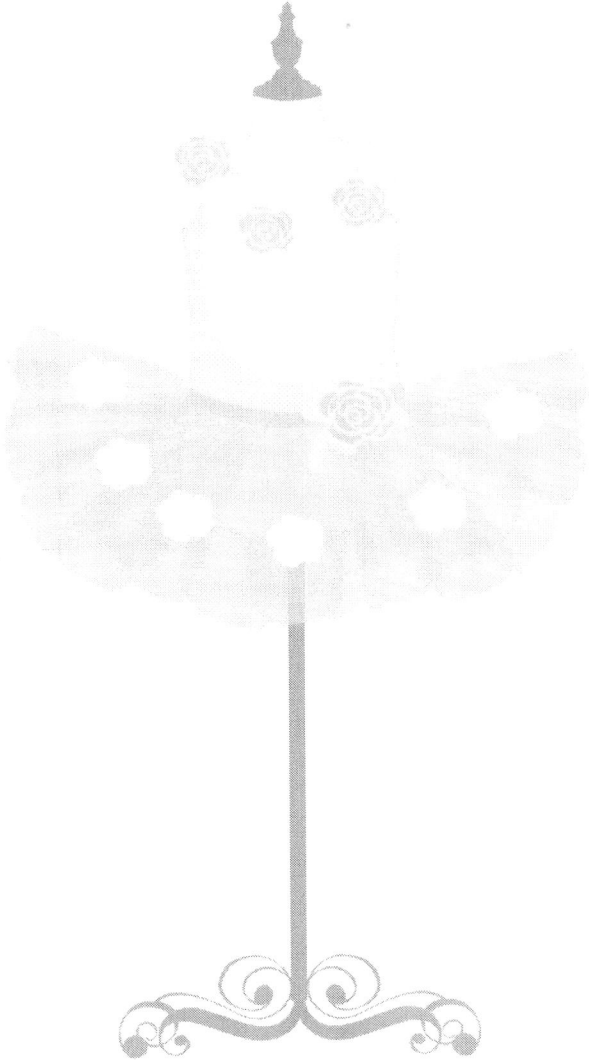

My Dancing Goals

GOAL:	What Do I Need To Do:	✓

GOAL:	What Do I Need To Do:	✓

GOAL:	What Do I Need To Do:	✓

Weekly Dance Plan

MON:

TUE:

WED:

THUR:

FRI:

SAT:

SUN:

PREPARATION

NOTES

THOUGHTS

My Lesson

LESSON DATE:

TEACHER:

ROUTINE:

LESSON FOCUS:

RESULTS: ✓

WHAT WENT WELL:

THINGS I NEED TO WORK ON:

My Practice Plan

MON	
TUE	
WED	
THUR	
FRI	
SAT	
SUN	

My Dance Practice

DATE

ROUTINE:

WHAT TO FOCUS ON:

WHAT WAS GOING WELL:

FEELINGS ABOUT ROUTINE:

WHERE DO I NEED TO IMPROVE:

NOTES:

THOUGHTS AND REFELECTIONS:

My Dance Practice

DATE

ROUTINE:

WHAT TO FOCUS ON:

WHAT WAS GOING WELL:

FEELINGS ABOUT ROUTINE:

WHERE DO I NEED TO IMPROVE:

NOTES:

THOUGHTS AND REFELECTIONS:

My Dance Practice

DATE

WHAT TO FOCUS ON:

FEELINGS ABOUT ROUTINE:

THOUGHTS AND REFELECTIONS:

ROUTINE:

WHAT WAS GOING WELL:

WHERE DO I NEED TO IMPROVE:

NOTES:

My Dance Practice

DATE

ROUTINE:

WHAT TO FOCUS ON:

WHAT WAS GOING WELL:

FEELINGS ABOUT ROUTINE:

WHERE DO I NEED TO IMPROVE:

NOTES:

THOUGHTS AND REFELECTIONS:

Self-Care Planner

TASKS & ERRANDS
MON:
TUES:
WED:
THUR:
FRI:
SAT:
SUN:

TO DO LIST:

NOTES & REMINDERS

THOUGHTS

Future Goals

WHEN	MY GOALS	STEPS
6 MONTHS		
1 YEAR		
2 YEARS		
5 YEARS		

WHERE I CAN DRAW INSPIRATION FROM:

Checklist

FOR: DATE: ✓

NOTES:

I love Dance Because..

My Dancing Goals

GOAL:	What Do I Need To Do:	✔

GOAL:	What Do I Need To Do:	✔

GOAL:	What Do I Need To Do:	✔

Weekly Dance Plan

MON:

TUE:

WED:

THUR:

FRI:

SAT:

SUN:

PREPARATION

NOTES

THOUGHTS

My Lesson

LESSON DATE:

TEACHER:

ROUTINE:

LESSON FOCUS:

RESULTS: ✓

WHAT WENT WELL:

THINGS I NEED TO WORK ON:

My Practice Plan

MON	
TUE	
WED	
THUR	
FRI	
SAT	
SUN	

My Dance Practice

DATE

ROUTINE:

WHAT TO FOCUS ON:

WHAT WAS GOING WELL:

FEELINGS ABOUT ROUTINE:

WHERE DO I NEED TO IMPROVE:

NOTES:

THOUGHTS AND REFELECTIONS:

My Dance Practice

DATE

ROUTINE:

WHAT TO FOCUS ON:

WHAT WAS GOING WELL:

FEELINGS ABOUT ROUTINE:

WHERE DO I NEED TO IMPROVE:

NOTES:

THOUGHTS AND REFELECTIONS:

My Dance Practice

DATE

WHAT TO FOCUS ON:

FEELINGS ABOUT ROUTINE:

THOUGHTS AND REFELECTIONS:

ROUTINE:

WHAT WAS GOING WELL:

WHERE DO I NEED TO IMPROVE:

NOTES:

My Dance Practice

DATE

ROUTINE:

WHAT TO FOCUS ON:

WHAT WAS GOING WELL:

FEELINGS ABOUT ROUTINE:

WHERE DO I NEED TO IMPROVE:

NOTES:

THOUGHTS AND REFELECTIONS:

Self-Care Planner

TASKS & ERRANDS

MON:

TUES:

WED:

THUR:

FRI:

SAT:

SUN:

TO DO LIST:

NOTES & REMINDERS

THOUGHTS

Future Goals

WHEN	MY GOALS	STEPS
6 MONTHS		
1 YEAR		
2 YEARS		
5 YEARS		

WHERE I CAN DRAW INSPIRATION FROM:

Checklist

FOR: _____ DATE: _____ ✓

_____ _____ ☐

_____ _____ ☐

_____ _____ ☐

_____ _____ ☐

_____ _____ ☐

_____ _____ ☐

_____ _____ ☐

_____ _____ ☐

_____ _____ ☐

_____ _____ ☐

_____ _____ ☐

_____ _____ ☐

_____ _____ ☐

_____ _____ ☐

_____ _____ ☐

NOTES:

I love Dance Because..

My Dancing Goals

GOAL:	What Do I Need To Do:	✓

GOAL:	What Do I Need To Do:	✓

GOAL:	What Do I Need To Do:	✓

Weekly Dance Plan

MON:

TUE:

WED:

THUR:

FRI:

SAT:

SUN:

PREPARATION

NOTES

THOUGHTS

My Lesson

LESSON DATE:

TEACHER:

ROUTINE:

LESSON FOCUS:

RESULTS: ✓

WHAT WENT WELL:

THINGS I NEED TO WORK ON:

My Practice Plan

MON	
TUE	
WED	
THUR	
FRI	
SAT	
SUN	

My Dance Practice

DATE

ROUTINE:

WHAT TO FOCUS ON:

WHAT WAS GOING WELL:

FEELINGS ABOUT ROUTINE:

WHERE DO I NEED TO IMPROVE:

NOTES:

THOUGHTS AND REFELECTIONS:

My Dance Practice

DATE

ROUTINE:

WHAT TO FOCUS ON:

WHAT WAS GOING WELL:

FEELINGS ABOUT ROUTINE:

WHERE DO I NEED TO IMPROVE:

NOTES:

THOUGHTS AND REFELECTIONS:

My Dance Practice

DATE

ROUTINE:

WHAT TO FOCUS ON:

WHAT WAS GOING WELL:

FEELINGS ABOUT ROUTINE:

WHERE DO I NEED TO IMPROVE:

NOTES:

THOUGHTS AND REFELECTIONS:

My Dance Practice

DATE

ROUTINE:

WHAT TO FOCUS ON:

WHAT WAS GOING WELL:

FEELINGS ABOUT ROUTINE:

WHERE DO I NEED TO IMPROVE:

NOTES:

THOUGHTS AND REFELECTIONS:

Self-Care Planner

TASKS & ERRANDS

MON:

TUES:

WED:

THUR:

FRI:

SAT:

SUN:

TO DO LIST:

NOTES & REMINDERS

THOUGHTS

Future Goals

WHEN	MY GOALS	STEPS
6 MONTHS		
1 YEAR		
2 YEARS		
5 YEARS		

WHERE I CAN DRAW INSPIRATION FROM:

Checklist

FOR: _____   DATE: _____   ✓

_____   _____   ☐
_____   _____   ☐
_____   _____   ☐
_____   _____   ☐
_____   _____   ☐
_____   _____   ☐
_____   _____   ☐
_____   _____   ☐
_____   _____   ☐
_____   _____   ☐
_____   _____   ☐
_____   _____   ☐
_____   _____   ☐
_____   _____   ☐
_____   _____   ☐

NOTES:

I love Dance Because..

My Dancing Goals

GOAL:	What Do I Need To Do:	✓

GOAL:	What Do I Need To Do:	✓

GOAL:	What Do I Need To Do:	✓

Weekly Dance Plan

MON:

TUE:

WED:

THUR:

FRI:

SAT:

SUN:

PREPARATION

NOTES

THOUGHTS

My Lesson

LESSON DATE:

TEACHER:

ROUTINE:

LESSON FOCUS:

RESULTS: ✓

☐

☐

☐

☐

WHAT WENT WELL:

THINGS I NEED TO WORK ON:

When I Dance – I Feel....

My Dancing Goals

GOAL:	What Do I Need To Do:	✓

GOAL:	What Do I Need To Do:	✓

GOAL:	What Do I Need To Do:	✓

Weekly Dance Plan

MON:

TUE:

WED:

THUR:

FRI:

SAT:

SUN:

PREPARATION

NOTES

THOUGHTS

My Lesson

LESSON DATE:

TEACHER:

ROUTINE:

LESSON FOCUS:

RESULTS: ✓

WHAT WENT WELL:

THINGS I NEED TO WORK ON:

My Practice Plan

MON	
TUE	
WED	
THUR	
FRI	
SAT	
SUN	

My Dance Practice

DATE

ROUTINE:

WHAT TO FOCUS ON:

WHAT WAS GOING WELL:

FEELINGS ABOUT ROUTINE:

WHERE DO I NEED TO IMPROVE:

NOTES:

THOUGHTS AND REFELECTIONS:

My Dance Practice

DATE

WHAT TO FOCUS ON:

FEELINGS ABOUT ROUTINE:

THOUGHTS AND REFELECTIONS:

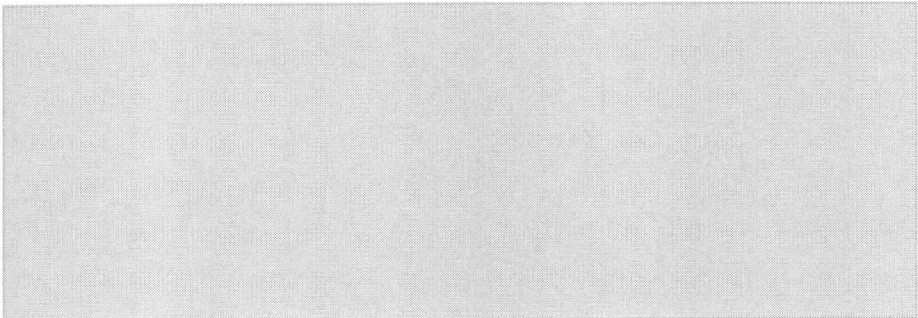

ROUTINE:

WHAT WAS GOING WELL:

WHERE DO I NEED TO IMPROVE:

NOTES:

My Dance Practice

DATE

ROUTINE:

WHAT TO FOCUS ON:

WHAT WAS GOING WELL:

FEELINGS ABOUT ROUTINE:

WHERE DO I NEED TO IMPROVE:

NOTES:

THOUGHTS AND REFELECTIONS:

My Dance Practice

DATE

ROUTINE:

WHAT TO FOCUS ON:

WHAT WAS GOING WELL:

FEELINGS ABOUT ROUTINE:

WHERE DO I NEED TO IMPROVE:

NOTES:

THOUGHTS AND REFELECTIONS:

Self-Care Planner

TASKS & ERRANDS	TO DO LIST:

MON:

TUES:

WED:

THUR:

FRI:

SAT:

SUN:

NOTES & REMINDERS

THOUGHTS

Future Goals

WHEN	MY GOALS	STEPS
6 MONTHS		
1 YEAR		
2 YEARS		
5 YEARS		

WHERE I CAN DRAW INSPIRATION FROM:

Checklist

FOR: DATE: ✓

NOTES:

I love Dance Because..

My Dancing Goals

GOAL:	What Do I Need To Do:	✓

GOAL:	What Do I Need To Do:	✓

GOAL:	What Do I Need To Do:	✓

Weekly Dance Plan

MON:

TUE:

WED:

THUR:

FRI:

SAT:

SUN:

PREPARATION

NOTES

THOUGHTS

My Lesson

LESSON DATE:

TEACHER:

ROUTINE:

LESSON FOCUS:

RESULTS: ✓

WHAT WENT WELL:

THINGS I NEED TO WORK ON:

My Practice Plan

MON	
TUE	
WED	
THUR	
FRI	
SAT	
SUN	

My Dance Practice

DATE

ROUTINE:

WHAT TO FOCUS ON:

WHAT WAS GOING WELL:

FEELINGS ABOUT ROUTINE:

WHERE DO I NEED TO IMPROVE:

NOTES:

THOUGHTS AND REFELECTIONS:

My Dance Practice

DATE

WHAT TO FOCUS ON:

FEELINGS ABOUT ROUTINE:

THOUGHTS AND REFELECTIONS:

ROUTINE:

WHAT WAS GOING WELL:

WHERE DO I NEED TO IMPROVE:

NOTES:

My Dance Practice

DATE

ROUTINE:

WHAT TO FOCUS ON:

WHAT WAS GOING WELL:

FEELINGS ABOUT ROUTINE:

WHERE DO I NEED TO IMPROVE:

NOTES:

THOUGHTS AND REFELECTIONS:

My Dance Practice

DATE

ROUTINE:

WHAT TO FOCUS ON:

WHAT WAS GOING WELL:

FEELINGS ABOUT ROUTINE:

WHERE DO I NEED TO IMPROVE:

NOTES:

THOUGHTS AND REFELECTIONS:

Self-Care Planner

TASKS & ERRANDS

MON:

TUES:

WED:

THUR:

FRI:

SAT:

SUN:

TO DO LIST:

NOTES & REMINDERS

THOUGHTS

Future Goals

WHEN	MY GOALS	STEPS
6 MONTHS		
1 YEAR		
2 YEARS		
5 YEARS		

WHERE I CAN DRAW INSPIRATION FROM:

Checklist

FOR: _____   DATE: _____   ✓

_____   _____   ☐
_____   _____   ☐
_____   _____   ☐
_____   _____   ☐
_____   _____   ☐
_____   _____   ☐
_____   _____   ☐
_____   _____   ☐
_____   _____   ☐
_____   _____   ☐
_____   _____   ☐
_____   _____   ☐
_____   _____   ☐
_____   _____   ☐
_____   _____   ☐

NOTES:

I love Dance Because..

My Dancing Goals

GOAL:	What Do I Need To Do:	✔

GOAL:	What Do I Need To Do:	✔

GOAL:	What Do I Need To Do:	✔

Weekly Dance Plan

MON:

TUE:

WED:

THUR:

FRI:

SAT:

SUN:

PREPARATION

NOTES

THOUGHTS

My Lesson

LESSON DATE:

TEACHER:

ROUTINE:

LESSON FOCUS:

RESULTS: ✓

WHAT WENT WELL:

THINGS I NEED TO WORK ON:

My Practice Plan

MON	
TUE	
WED	
THUR	
FRI	
SAT	
SUN	

My Dance Practice

DATE

ROUTINE:

WHAT TO FOCUS ON:

WHAT WAS GOING WELL:

WHERE DO I NEED TO IMPROVE:

FEELINGS ABOUT ROUTINE:

NOTES:

THOUGHTS AND REFELECTIONS:

My Dance Practice

DATE

WHAT TO FOCUS ON:

FEELINGS ABOUT ROUTINE:

THOUGHTS AND REFELECTIONS:

ROUTINE:

WHAT WAS GOING WELL:

WHERE DO I NEED TO IMPROVE:

NOTES:

My Dance Practice

DATE

ROUTINE:

WHAT TO FOCUS ON:

WHAT WAS GOING WELL:

WHERE DO I NEED TO IMPROVE:

FEELINGS ABOUT ROUTINE:

NOTES:

THOUGHTS AND REFELECTIONS:

My Dance Practice

DATE

ROUTINE:

WHAT TO FOCUS ON:

WHAT WAS GOING WELL:

FEELINGS ABOUT ROUTINE:

WHERE DO I NEED TO IMPROVE:

NOTES:

THOUGHTS AND REFELECTIONS:

Self-Care Planner

TASKS & ERRANDS

MON:

TUES:

WED:

THUR:

FRI:

SAT:

SUN:

TO DO LIST:

NOTES & REMINDERS

THOUGHTS

Future Goals

WHEN	MY GOALS	STEPS
6 MONTHS		
1 YEAR		
2 YEARS		
5 YEARS		

WHERE I CAN DRAW INSPIRATION FROM:

Checklist

FOR: DATE: ✓

NOTES:

I love Dance Because..

My Dancing Goals

GOAL:	What Do I Need To Do:	✔

GOAL:	What Do I Need To Do:	✔

GOAL:	What Do I Need To Do:	✔

Weekly Dance Plan

MON:

TUE:

WED:

THUR:

FRI:

SAT:

SUN:

PREPARATION

NOTES

THOUGHTS

My Lesson

LESSON DATE:

TEACHER:

ROUTINE:

LESSON FOCUS:

RESULTS: ✓

WHAT WENT WELL:

THINGS I NEED TO WORK ON:

My Practice Plan

MON	
TUE	
WED	
THUR	
FRI	
SAT	
SUN	

My Dance Practice

DATE

ROUTINE:

WHAT TO FOCUS ON:

WHAT WAS GOING WELL:

WHERE DO I NEED TO IMPROVE:

FEELINGS ABOUT ROUTINE:

NOTES:

THOUGHTS AND REFELECTIONS:

My Dance Practice

DATE

WHAT TO FOCUS ON:

FEELINGS ABOUT ROUTINE:

THOUGHTS AND REFELECTIONS:

ROUTINE:

WHAT WAS GOING WELL:

WHERE DO I NEED TO IMPROVE:

NOTES:

My Dance Practice

DATE

ROUTINE:

WHAT TO FOCUS ON:

WHAT WAS GOING WELL:

WHERE DO I NEED TO IMPROVE:

FEELINGS ABOUT ROUTINE:

NOTES:

THOUGHTS AND REFELECTIONS:

My Dance Practice

DATE

WHAT TO FOCUS ON:

FEELINGS ABOUT ROUTINE:

THOUGHTS AND REFELECTIONS:

ROUTINE:

WHAT WAS GOING WELL:

WHERE DO I NEED TO IMPROVE:

NOTES:

Self-Care Planner

TASKS & ERRANDS

MON:

TUES:

WED:

THUR:

FRI:

SAT:

SUN:

TO DO LIST:

NOTES & REMINDERS

THOUGHTS

Future Goals

WHEN	MY GOALS	STEPS
6 MONTHS		
1 YEAR		
2 YEARS		
5 YEARS		

WHERE I CAN DRAW INSPIRATION FROM:

Checklist

FOR: _____   DATE: _____   ✓

_____   _____ ☐
_____   _____ ☐
_____   _____ ☐
_____   _____ ☐
_____   _____ ☐
_____   _____ ☐
_____   _____ ☐
_____   _____ ☐
_____   _____ ☐
_____   _____ ☐
_____   _____ ☐
_____   _____ ☐
_____   _____ ☐
_____   _____ ☐
_____   _____ ☐

NOTES:

I love Dance Because..

My Dancing Goals

GOAL:	What Do I Need To Do:	✓

GOAL:	What Do I Need To Do:	✓

GOAL:	What Do I Need To Do:	✓

Weekly Dance Plan

MON:

TUE:

WED:

THUR:

FRI:

SAT:

SUN:

PREPARATION

NOTES

THOUGHTS

My Lesson

LESSON DATE:

TEACHER:

ROUTINE:

LESSON FOCUS:

RESULTS: ✓

WHAT WENT WELL:

THINGS I NEED TO WORK ON:

My Practice Plan

MON	
TUE	
WED	
THUR	
FRI	
SAT	
SUN	

My Dance Practice

DATE

WHAT TO FOCUS ON:

FEELINGS ABOUT ROUTINE:

THOUGHTS AND REFELECTIONS:

ROUTINE:

WHAT WAS GOING WELL:

WHERE DO I NEED TO IMPROVE:

NOTES:

My Dance Practice

DATE

WHAT TO FOCUS ON:

FEELINGS ABOUT ROUTINE:

THOUGHTS AND REFELECTIONS:

ROUTINE:

WHAT WAS GOING WELL:

WHERE DO I NEED TO IMPROVE:

NOTES:

My Dance Practice

DATE

ROUTINE:

WHAT TO FOCUS ON:

WHAT WAS GOING WELL:

FEELINGS ABOUT ROUTINE:

WHERE DO I NEED TO IMPROVE:

NOTES:

THOUGHTS AND REFELECTIONS:

My Dance Practice

DATE

WHAT TO FOCUS ON:

FEELINGS ABOUT ROUTINE:

THOUGHTS AND REFELECTIONS:

ROUTINE:

WHAT WAS GOING WELL:

WHERE DO I NEED TO IMPROVE:

NOTES:

Self-Care Planner

TASKS & ERRANDS
MON:
TUES:
WED:
THUR:
FRI:
SAT:
SUN:

TO DO LIST:

NOTES & REMINDERS

THOUGHTS

Future Goals

WHEN	MY GOALS	STEPS
6 MONTHS		
1 YEAR		
2 YEARS		
5 YEARS		

WHERE I CAN DRAW INSPIRATION FROM:

Checklist

FOR: DATE: ✓

NOTES:

I love Dance Because..

Made in the USA
Las Vegas, NV
26 September 2021